# Castle Combe to Malmesbury

## IN OLD PHOTOGRAPHS

A "Style" much in favour at Malmesbury. I've tried it.

This postcard, postmarked 7 July 1908, purports to show the idyllic life to be enjoyed in the countryside around Malmesbury. Although the stile may have vanished, 'Malmesbury style' hasn't!

# Castle Combe to Malmesbury

## IN OLD PHOTOGRAPHS

*Collected by*
ANNETTE WILSON
*and* MIKE WILSON

Alan Sutton Publishing Limited
Phoenix Mill · Far Thrupp
Stroud · Gloucestershire

First published 1992

Copyright © Annette Wilson and
Mike Wilson, 1992

British Library Cataloguing
in Publication Data

Wilson, Annette
Around Malmesbury in Old Photographs
I. Title II. Wilson, Mike
942.312

ISBN 0-7509-0101-2

Typeset in 9/10 Sabon.
Typesetting and origination by
Alan Sutton Publishing Limited
Printed in Great Britain by
WBC Print Ltd, Bridgend.

Sadly, we have to dedicate this book to
Phyllis Matthews, who was a great friend to
both of us and who died in July of this year.
Phyl had an enormous circle of friends and
was a wonderful source of local information.
She accompanied Annette on many of the
visits to the people who have kindly lent us
photographs and took great pleasure in all
the chat that took place, especially as many
of the contributors turned out to be old
acquaintances of hers. We only wish that she
had seen the completion of the book in
which she took such an interest. This was
her favourite photograph of herself and featured in our book *Chippenham and Lacock
in Old Photographs*.

# Contents

Richard Jeffries, who was employed by Mr Knight on Barrow Farm, Langley Burrell, epitomizes Wiltshire village life in 1925. He died at the age of 82 years.

# Introduction

This book is an attempt to illustrate the traditions and industries which thrived in North Wiltshire in days gone by. It covers an area centred on Castle Combe, reputed to be the most beautiful village in Britain, and Malmesbury, the oldest borough, and includes the communities around those places, from Colerne to Easton Grey. The core of the area was designated part of the Cotswold Area of Outstanding Beauty in 1966, but it is a matter for debate locally whether this is true 'Cotswold' country.

Much of the scenery in this part of Wiltshire has remained unchanged but the fashions, vehicles and disposables of life, here as elsewhere, have changed with time's passage. Many of the villages have lost their character – through road widening, for example. Village greens have disappeared along with village ponds, the need for which has gone now that horse-drawn vehicles have been replaced by petrol-driven ones and the drover by the lorry.

Malmesbury, possessor of the oldest borough charter, has many historical associations, and its importance in the county cannot be ignored, but in this type of book it can only be touched upon. The whole area has been a favourite with the kings and queens of the realm from very early times right up to the modern day.

There will no doubt be inaccuracies, as memories, sources of most of the information, are sadly fallible. But if there are any names, dates or corrections that you can contribute, we should be only too happy to learn of them. Our apologies to anyone whose material has not been used, but we have been inundated with beautiful photographs and the selection process has, as always, been enormously difficult. We would like to thank family and friends, and especially Christine, Sandi and Jenny for their help with the typing and for not disowning us yet.

## CASTLE COMBE AND MALMESBURY

Castle Combe's name derives from the castle built by the family of Walter de Dunstanville whose tomb in the village church has his effigy in chain mail, a memorial to mark his death in 1270. The castle has long since disappeared from the hill overlooking the present village. It was, at one time, a small market town with the two or three cloth mills usually found in those little towns that had the advantage of running water. In this case the river has since been reduced to a picturesque trout stream. There is evidence of pre-Norman habitation, albeit scanty, the Fosse Way runs along the north western boundary of the area, and there are evidences of Roman occupation, such as coins and fragments of sculpture.

Castle Combe was conveyed to Reginald de Dunstanville in the reign of Henry I by his wife, Adeliza, and the castle was probably built around this time. The ownership of the Manor of Castle Combe changed hands many times during the years that followed until, in 1375, in the reign of Edward III, the wardship of the three infant heiresses of Sir Robert de Tibetot was sold to Sir Richard Scrope for 1,000 marks. By betrothing the three girls to his sons, he secured the large estates involved for his own family. It seems that one of his sons, Nicholas, had died, as his betrothed was later married to Philip de Despenser.

Castle Combe was on the pilgrim's route to Glastonbury, and a statue of St James, the patron saint of pilgrims, is one of six saints portrayed in the central arch of the parish church.

A *Eulogy of Histories*, written around 1366, possibly by a monk of Malmesbury, records that a monk named Maidulph came from Ireland and after wandering around for some time settled near the castle of Bladon, called Ingleburne by the Saxons, built around the year 642 near the site of the present town of Malmesbury. There was a royal residence at Cairdurburgh, which is now called Brokenborough, and there Maidulph built a hermitage beneath the castle. Later he gathered some scholars and started a school. Aldhelm grew up in this community, went to Canterbury where he continued his studies, then returned to Malmesbury where be became a monk. He became Abbot of Malmesbury and was Bishop of Sherborne. Being of royal descent, he brought many benefactors to the Abbey of Malmesbury. He died in 709 and is buried at Malmesbury.

After William de Colerne became Abbot, in 1260, he was responsible for many improvements to the Abbey and drew up rules to ensure all the monks were treated equally. The story of Elmer, the monk who fixed wings to his hands and feet and jumped from a tower, is well known: he 'flew' for a furlong before crashing to the ground and breaking both his legs, then said his failure was caused by his not providing himelf with a tail! A window in the Abbey records the event.

King Alfred's grandson, Athelstan, first King of all England, has a tomb in the Abbey but his grave is unknown. In 937 Athelstan went to battle and settled there and then who would be overall ruler three years later. King's Heath is named for Athelstan; he gave the common of 500 acres to the people, every freeman of Athelstan's borough being entitled to one allotment. Until the beginning of the eighteenth century any male inhabitant of Malmesbury could become a commoner, but in 1727 the burgesses passed new rules permitting only sons, sons-in-law and apprentices to become commoners; in 1821 the apprentices were omitted. A publication called *The Old Corporation of Malmesbury*, printed and published by the Trustees of the Old Corporation, has a most interesting and full history of the Borough Charter.

# SECTION ONE

# Locations

This picture postcard of Castle Combe is captioned 'A Roman Village', and evidence of Roman occupation has been discovered, which is not surprising as the beautiful site is bounded on the north west by the Roman road known as the Fosse Way. The character of the village has changed very little since this picture was taken at the turn of the century. Missing are the Deer Gates, just discernible above the arches of the bridge and, of course, the smoke from the chimneys.

Aerial view of Castle Combe market place, probably from around the turn of the century. The field behind the houses is now heavily wooded.

Castle Combe market with the parish church of St Andrew in the background.

The bridge over By Brook, looking down the road towards Ford. Both of these pictures are taken from postcards on sale in the early years of this century.

An old picture of Burton, showing the sign of the Old House and Home Inn and the garage opposite. Burton lies in a dip at the head of By Brook, and though it is a tiny village of grey stone cottages it boasts two inns; the other one is the Plume of Feathers. With Nettleton and West Kington, Burton is one of three communities making up the parish of Nettleton.

Green Farm, Nettleton. The pond in the foreground has since been grassed over. Nettleton itself is a sprawl of cottages along several minor roads. In a field off the Fosse Way is one of the oldest monuments in England: three large stones which were once an arch on a grassy mound mark the communal grave of many warriors.

Tutten Hill, part of old Colerne. Sir Walter Raleigh once lived at Euridge Farm near Colerne. The village is situated 400 feet above By Brook on the edge of the dip slope of the Cotswolds. Its position made it ideal for an RAF station, so much so that Fighter Command continued at Colerne until 1976. Much of the village was built in the last thirty years and so it is often regarded as a modern creation, but our modern village has very old roots. Colerne was held by Leofnoth and valued at £10 according to the Domesday Book, and the Abbey records at Malmesbury show William de Colerne was Abbot from 1260 until his death in 1296.

Slaughterford church was founded by Empress Matilda but fell into disrepair and was a ruin for 200 years until it was rescued and restored. Some people think that Slaughterford is named after a great battle, but most books agree it derives from Slacktoneford, as it is given on the assize roll of 1176. Slacktorn means sloe bush, so this is the ford by the sloe bush. Sloes were and are much prized locally for making remedial wines and for flavouring sloe gin.

Ford lies on the Bristol Road between Chippenham and Marshfield. Behind the trees on the right are several cottages and two farms. A lane runs up the hill beside the chapel, where there are more cottages. The White Hart Inn is beside the small cottage on the left. Deep in the valley of the By Brook, this small Cotswold village marks a major crossing point for the A420 Bristol Road. Wraxall parish comprises North Wraxall, Upper Wraxall, The Shoe, Mountain Bower and Ford.

Biddestone's 1187 spelling is Bedeneston and probably derives from the personal name Biedin; this may mark the site of his farm or tun. In the Domesday Book Bedestone, as it is called, was valued at just 20s and was owned by Humphrey who held Castle Combe and was held from him by Thorketel. This picture is of Biddestone war memorial, on the edge of the village green, and a small group of the beautiful houses that make Biddestone such a jewel. The village pond and green, fronted by well maintained eighteenth-century cottages, make this one of the most picturesque and unspoilt villages in the area.

Yatton Keynell Baptist chapel, built in 1835. Yatton Keynell's name may derive from Henry Caynel, who had a holding in the area in 1242, and from the original name in 1086 of Getone (Yatton), or Geat 'Gap' which is the head of the well-marked valley to the west of the village.

Jim Hulance (right) enjoying a pint outside The Red Lion in Grittleton, probably during the 1930s. The Red Lion later became The Neeld Arms and is now closed and up for sale. Grittleton's name is of difficult origin, but there are two possibilities: Grytels Farm, or, as Ekwall suggests, *Greothlinc* or 'gravel hill', thus Gravel Hill Farm.

The Almshouses, Kington St Michael, given to the old folk of his birthplace by Isaac Lyte after he became an Alderman of London. Isaac Lyte was christened in the church of St Michael and All Angels, Kington St Michael.

Tom Hazel (in dark suit) driving a cow past Hullavington pond, which no longer exists, in the mid-1920s. His parents, Mr and Mrs J. Hazel kept The Star Inn in the village. Hullavington's name is thought to derive from Hundlaf's or Hunlaf's Farm. William Collingbourne, who lived here, was hanged for writing two short lines about Richard III to which the King took exception: 'The cat, the rat and Lovel the dog/Rule all England under the hog.'

Luckington, where the Bristol Avon has its source, has a twelfth-century church dedicated to St Mary and St Ethelbert (of Kent). One of the windows shows William of Malmesbury holding a church. William, one-time Abbot of Malmesbury, was one of the earliest historians and chroniclers. Luckington Manor, shown here in 1929, was the home of Rear Admiral Sir Reginald Neeld, brother of Sir Audley Neeld of Grittleton.

Knockdown, Sherston. Sherston is thought to derive from *Sceorston*, scora meaning steep slope and stan, rock or stone. John Rattlebone is said to have fought the Danes here in 1016 with Edmund Ironside. Sherston has a long history. There are signs of old earthworks beside the church of the Holy Cross which dates back at least 900 years. Mention was made in the Domesday Book of a Saxon church here but no remains have been found. The church had a ring of five bells until 1977, when they were re-hung and the opportunity taken to complete a ring of six.

Easton Grey is a collection of Cotswold-style cottages on the bank of the Avon. The name derives from East Farm which belonged to John de Grey in 1243. The Manor belonged to the Parry family in the seventeenth century and they are commemorated in the church, the tower of which is now some 650 years old.

Westonbirt House. Sir Robert Stayner Holford, born in 1808, was the builder of the present house. In 1829 he began planting the Arboretum before he became Lord of the Manor in 1892. Sir George Holford, his son, continued his interest with the Arboretum. It is said that George would consider the position for a new tree for anything up to three weeks. After his death his nephew sold the house but kept the Arboretum. The house became a public school for girls, opened by the Duke of Beaufort on Friday 11 May 1928. The church was built fifty years after the Domesday survey was made, and dedicated to St Catherine of Alexandria, whose emblem is the wheel and the dagger. She is the patron saint of young women and education.

Charlton House lies within a park of some 600 acres. It is of Elizabethan origin but was refashioned in the eighteenth century. The poet Dryden fell in love with Lady Elizabeth Howard, daughter of the household, and their first son was later born there. Dryden originally came to Charlton in 1665, while in his early 30s, to take refuge from the Plague and the war. Charlton House later became the home of the Earl of Suffolk. The name Charlton derives from *Cherleton*, Farm of the Churls, or free peasants.

Pinkney lies just east of Sherston and was the manor of Ralph de Pinkenny in 1201. The Avon flows through Pinkney Park towards Malmesbury through a countryside of copses and walled fields.

An unusual view of Malmesbury market place, with the market cross in the foreground and the Abbey dominating the background. The ivy covered building in front of the Abbey was the town hospital. On the left is the shop of T. Day, purveyor.

Malmesbury High Street at the turn of the century, with the Abbey making an imposing backdrop.

Malmesbury seen from the far side of the River Avon and Daniels Well. On the skyline is the tower of St Mary's church with the ruins of the Abbey to the right of it.

The King's Arms Hotel, Malmesbury, with the landlord, Mr Harry Jones, with top hat and buttonhole, standing before the coach arch.

Bell Hotel, Malmesbury. The style of the car in the foreground suggests that the photograph was taken between 1910 and 1920.

Burton Hill House, Malmesbury, a private residence until 1946 when it was bought by the Shaftesbury Society to establish a pioneer school for severely handicapped girls. Originally, only children with spina bifida were admitted, but by 1976, when J.S. Pollard was headmaster. Miss P.A. Ludlow Hewitt took over as matron from Muriel Northcott, who left to become Mrs Stanley Hadlow, boys and girls with different disabilities were accepted. In 1952 Miss Green started Burton Hill's own guide company and in 1976 Jackie Bowkett became the first disabled Queens Guide in Malmesbury.

Tetbury during a particularly fierce thunderstorm. The Town Hall at Tetbury has stood since 1665 and has looked exactly as it does now since 1815. The church is perhaps Tetbury's biggest surprise to the visitor: it looks grand and impressive without, and yet it is chapel-like inside, with a roof supported by over 100 wooden poles.

Looking down Cutwell Hill from the corner of West Street, Tetbury, 1950. This picture was used on a postcard some forty years ago. The shop on the corner, which used to be run by Mrs Eldridge, has long since closed. All the land behind Ivy Cottage, in the middle distance, has been built on, as has the area beside the telegraph pole on the right.

Street Farm, Little Somerford. The Sloper family have assembled for this enchanting portrait. Their association with the farm ended in the 1930s. The name Somerford means just that: a ford which is passable during the summer months. Little Somerford and Great Somerford are separated by half a mile of meadowland across which passed the summer ford. The villages are very different in character. Little Somerford centres on a crossroad, whereas Great Somerford is loosely gathered together on a network of lanes.

Seagry House, home of Clare, Countess Cowley, Upper Seagry. The name was originally Segrie in 1086 and probably derives from *Seeg-rio*, which means sedge-stream. The villages were called Over and Nether Seagry at the time but are now known as Upper and Lower.

His Supreme Highness Prince Franz von Hatzfeldt-Weldenburg in the grounds of Draycott House, which he leased from Earl Cowley until his death on 3 November 1910. A memorial service was held at St James's church, Draycott Cerne by Revd R.L.A. Westlake. This took place at the same time as his funeral at Crottorf in the Rhineland, on 9 November. Earlier, a Requiem Mass was celebrated at the church of the Immaculate Conception, Farm Street, London by the Very Reverend Father Charles Nicholson.

The Doctors Surgery, Sutton Benger before it became the Bell House Hotel. Doctors Sturridge, Sawden, Spong and Robinson were the GPs at this time. Sutton Benger is thought to mean the South Farm of Berenger who was under tenant in the fourteenth century.

The General Stores, Christian Malford, owned by Edward and Evelyn Kite. Standing outside the shop doorway are Mrs Kite, on the left, and Nellie Clark, who assisted in the shop. Groceries were delivered by trade bike when requested. Christian Malford's name comes from *Cristel Mael* meaning Ford by a Cross.

Dauntsey House, owned at present by the Sturgess family, but throughout the sixteenth century by the Danvers family, notably Henry Danvers, 1st Earl of Danby, who established the Almshouses, and Sir John Danvers and Lady Jane, whose memorial brasses are in the parish church along with the 'Dauntsey Doom', which was once above the chancel and represents the Last Judgement.

The Jolly Trooper at Bradenstoke, where Mr Baker was the landlord in the 1920s. Mr and Mrs Iles lived in the second cottage from the left with their family at this time. Bradenstoke once boasted a Priory which was built in the eleventh century. It was demolished and all the stonework and timbers removed in 1930 and taken to St Donat's Castle in Glamorgan. Mr Storey, a local millionaire, gave a Christmas party for the village children in 1920, complete with Christmas tree, a conjuror and other entertainment. It took place in the Priory crypt.

# SECTION TWO

# Children and Schools

This little girl peering through the gateway into the drive which led to Mr Eels Dairy in Castle Combe epitomizes the peacefulness of village life at the turn of the century. The outbuildings in this picture have gone now, to make way for a bottling and pasteurizing plant, but the dairy is still flourishing.

Castle Combe School, *c.* 1925. Back row, left to right: -?-, -?-, John Eels, -?-, Burt Bristow, -?-, -?-, -?-, -?-. Third row: P. White, Marjorie Ayres, -?-, -?-, -?-, Freda Ayres, -?-, May Young, -?-, Jessie Bristow, Grace Eels, Vera Beazer, -?-, D. White. Second row: -?-, Lily Tuck, Molly Tuck, -?-, Sybil and Betty Preedy, -?-, -?-, Dorothy Ball, Beattie Haliday, Edith Eels, Sylvia Bristow, -?-, -?-. Front row: -?-, Chris Eels, -?-, Frank Eels, -?-, Frank Haliday, Viney Pullen, -?-, Emily Broom, Ethel Ponter, Kathy Pullen, -?-, Clifford White.

Castle Combe School, *c.* 1927. Front row, left to right: Clifford White, Guy Smith, Maurice Snell, -?-, -?-, Olive Haliday, Eric Snell, Jack Moore, Frank Gittus, -?-. Second row: Kathy Pullen, Violet Gittus, -?-, Renee Hanks, ? Pearce, Gladys White, Sylvie Tuck, Nancy Sheppard, -?-. Group behind Pearce: Johnny Gittus, Victor(?) Pullen, Rita Eels, Frank Haliday, Joan White. Third row: -?-, Jack White, Girlie Purbrick, Hector Whitmore, Emily Broom, Bill Gale, Flossie White, Viney Pullen, Beattie Haliday, Sylvia Bristow, Win Goodfellow, Dorothy Bale, -?-, Frank Eels, Chris Eels, -?-,. -?-, Freddie Purbrick. (The Purbrick family lived opposite the Gib and they walked to and from school each day.) The three children at centre back are not known.

The Laurels, Castle Combe (*c*. 1922), home of Albert and Ella Eels, of Eels Dairy, which was situated behind the house. In the garden are their children, Grace, Christopher and Rita.

Mike Wilson, his sister Jenny, and cousin Paul Squirrell, taking full advantage of the cool waters of the stream that runs by The Shoe, at the junction of the Bristol Road with the Fosse Way near North Wraxall, 1963.

Timothy, son of Albert and Eva Derrick, on the farm at Westend, Nettleton, 1953.

Joy Derrick, of Westend Farm, Nettleton, on her pony Silver around 1962. Joy would compete at local gymkhanas with Silver.

Nettleton School, 1954. Miss Cowley, the teacher, lived in the village. Back row, left to right: Jimmy Clark, -?-, Brenda Alsworth, Mike Packer, -?-, -?-, -?-. Middle row: Anne Alsworth, Lorna Wright(?), -?-, Dolly Packer, -?-, Denis Marsh, -?-, Wendy Rollings. Front row: John Wright, -?-, Nigel Selman, Tony Cleverly.

Hugh Brammer from Nottingham visiting Eva Ward and her brothers, Alan and Ted, Stanley Brammer and Jack Ward (in the tent!), with the woodshed of Manor Farm, Nettleton in the background.

Frank Young and his friend Norah Brewer (1928), playing with the farm cats from Elmtree Farm, Nettleton – where the Good quads lived after Mr and Mrs Brewer moved away. Frank was killed in the Second World War while serving in the Royal Navy.

Fred and Gordon Swan in the doorway of Westway Farm, Castle Combe, in the 1930s.

Katherine (Kitty) Billet, who lived with her aunt at Grittleton after the death of her mother in childbirth, when Kitty was only two years old. It was usual for children to be dressed in white for Whit Sunday, so her family think this is why she is so elaborately dressed in this 1908 picture.

Grittleton School infants, 1922. Front row, left to right: Elsie Banks, Alfred Bailey, Billy Gillam, George Wheeler, Roy Mann, Charlie Broom. Second row: -?-, Bessie Billett, Dorothy Broom, Bessie Elms, Lily Gainey, Christine Hulance, Florence Neate, Gladys Gillam, Lily Knott. Back row, from the left: Leslie Lewis, -?-, Reg Hopkins, Frank Avenell. The rest are unknown.

Grittleton School, 1926. Front row: Bill Gillam, Alfred Bailey, Reg Hopkins, Ted Rottenborough, Fred Billett, Gordon Archard, Frank Banks, Fred Hulance, Sidney Bailey, Roy Mann. Second row: Betty Archard, Christine Hulance, Bessie Billett, Bessie Elms, Florrie Bailey, Gladys Gillam.

Langley Burrell School, 1912. Among those pictured are: Gladys Clark, third from the left in the middle row, Dorothy Hunt, fifth from the left, Edith Payne, second from the right, and Violet Davis, fourth from left in the front row.

James Sage and his sister Agnes, the children of Kate and Frederick Sage of Moorshall Farm, pictured in 1916, in Kington St Michael.

On leaving the army James Wicks lived with his family in Luckington before they moved to Hullavington. This shows three of his daughters attending Hullavington School in around 1905. Nelly Wicks is seated first on the left, Phyllis is sixth and Dolly seventh. Note the lace decorating some girls' aprons.

Hullavington School, 1928. Front row, left to right: Mabel Greenman, Una Greenman, Marrion Fry, -?-, Jim Wicks, Molly Greenman, Jean Miles, Dorothy Smart, Edgar Jones, Mrs Ray. Middle row: Enid Wicks, Sylvia Peters, Helen Tanner, Bill Norris, Bert Greenman, -?-, Lucy Neal, Molly Tanner, -?-. Back row: Mr Ray, Eric Neate, Bob Jones, ? Edgington, Miss Price, M. Smart, Jim Chapel, Miss Lillywhite, Jim Chapel, Bob Tanner, Ethel Tanner, Tony Scrivener, G. Skull.

Luckington School, 1901. Geb Wicks is standing beside the schoolmaster on the right of the back row. His sister Gladys is third left in the third row, and two other sisters are in the second row, Nellie second from the left with arms folded, and Dolly fifth, beside the boy in the dark jacket.

Luckington School, around 1920. Most of the children's names are unknown, unfortunately, but Gabriel Wicks, who was killed in the First World War, is standing second right, in the back row. His sisters, Gladys and Dolly, are seated third and sixth from the left in the middle row, and Nellie is second from the left in the front row.

Dorothy, Frederick and Julia Young, posing with a trophy outside The Deerhouse, Badminton Park, where their father was gamekeeper to the Duke of Beaufort, 1914.

Rhoda Wilcox of Sherston (1877–1927) became a dairymaid at Hillsley, married William Henry Pritchard of Pinkney and had six children. Note the rag doll with wooden hands and feet, and the wooden chain, made after the style of Welsh love-spoons, around Rhoda's neck.

Emily Pritchard, dressed in 'white for Whit Sunday', 1899. (Note the cloth on the floor to keep her shoes clean!) Emily had beautiful auburn coloured hair and the creamy skin that goes with it. She was the eldest child of Harry and Rhoda Pritchard of Sherston.

The six children of Harry and Rhoda Pritchard, of Noble Street, Sherston, 1907. From the left: Denis, Eva, Louisa sitting on Emily's lap, William and Lilian.

John and Christopher Dore, in the garden behind the grocery shop their parents ran in the High Street, Sherston, *c.* 1937.

Malmesbury Infants' School (*c.* 1900) was situated in the Cross Hayes, where the library is now. Mrs May, the teacher, came from a musical family who would organize entertainments and concerts and gave music lessons. Edward (Ted) Barnes, who later joined his family's carpenters and undertakers business, is fourth from the left in the back row.

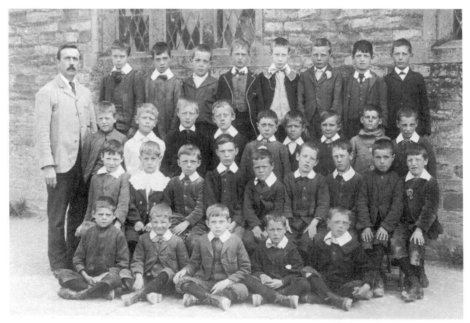

Westport Boys' School, 1902, situated in Gaston's Road, off the Bristol Road in Malmesbury. In recent times it has been used as an Art Centre. Edward Barnes is seated centre front. It is thought the teacher is Mr Clarke; the headmaster was known as 'Gaffer' Tinley.

Malmesbury Infants' School, July 1930. Back row, left to right: Sheila Laban, Frank Exton, Charley Scott, Peggy Pike. Middle row: Ken Haylock, -?-, Victor Weedon, -?-, -?-, Ron Fry. Front row: Kathleen Selby, Mavis Jones, Dorothy Barnes, Olinka Bowman.

*Lilac Time*, performed by Malmesbury Grammar School at Malmesbury Town Hall in May 1949. It was conducted by Miss Dean.

This photograph of the Webb children was taken at Lea School in 1932. At this time Mrs Prince was the headmistress and Miss Martin was a form teacher. From the left: Norman, Kath, Win, Dorothy, Edna and Ron.

Dolly Webb of Lea, who died of meningitis at the age of eight in 1939.

Harry Norris, in the garden of his home in Lewis Lane, Cirencester in 1925. After his marriage he lived at Cutwell, Tetbury.

Dorothy Bryl Barrett, of New Church Street, Tetbury, 1921. On leaving school Dorothy looked after William and Michael, the sons of Mr and Mrs George Gale, grocers of Long Street. Dorothy has lived all her life in Tetbury.

Tull's School in Tetbury, owned by Mr and Mrs Tull, closed when they moved to London in 1907. It was situated in Long Street. Mrs Letitia Barrett was cook at the school until it closed down.

Sutton Benger School, *c*. 1910. Blanche Thomas of Draycott Cerne is standing in the centre of the second row, wearing a white apron. Gladys Bevington, on the left of the same row and also wearing an apron, became Mrs Berridge. She was 92 years old in 1991.

Sandra Matthews and her cousin Sarah Bond in the garden of Lower Seagry Farm, with a view across the fields towards Upper Seagry, 1963.

Doris Lewis (centre) outside her cottage in Sutton Benger with Fred Hawkins and his sister Lilian, children of the local builder, 1928.

Betty Gainey, bridesmaid at the wedding of her aunt, Polly Duckett of Sutton Benger, around 1926. Betty's dress was pale pink, with a white overdress; her bouquet was a many coloured bunch of flowers gathered from the garden.

Mollie Hughes of Avonweir, Christian Malford, dressed as a Pierrette for the Christian Malford Fête, 10 July 1926.

Clive and Gordon Kite, choirboys at Christian Malford church, c. 1943. They were the sons of Edward and Evelyn Kite who ran the grocery shop in the village.

# SECTION THREE
# People

Mrs Ella Eels with her daughter, Grace, at Castle Combe, 1912.

Mr Joseph Swan of Westway Farm, Castle Combe, with his wife and ten children, 1915. Back row, left to right: Nan, who became companion to a doctor's wife, Joseph, who worked with his father on the farm, Winnie, Fred, who also worked on the farm, and Floss. Front row: Kathleen, a schoolteacher, Bert, who taught at Box School for many years, Mr Swan, Stanley, who was killed in a motor cycle accident, Mrs Hannah Swan, Bill and Dorothy. This picture was taken just before Joe went to the Dardanelles, in the First World War. He returned safely.

Mr Edwin (Ted) Eels, Mr Seymour Eels, Mrs Ethel Eels (wife of Edwin), Miss Georgina Eels and Mr Maurice Eels in the garden of Eastcombe Farm, Castle Combe in 1922.

The Marsh family moved from the Tormarton area to Nettleton after the Great Western Railway ran the main London–Bristol line through their land. The family then moved on to Yatton Keynell, where this picture was taken in approximately 1904. Standing, left to right: Charles Broom Marsh, Mary Sealy, Honor Jolliffe, Nathaniel William Marsh, John Archer Marsh. Seated: Edith Hulands, Nathaniel Bennett Marsh, Maria Tanner Marsh (his second wife), Annie Sheate.

Eva Ward and her brother, Ted, of Manor Farm, Nettleton, with their dogs, three of which were called Mickey, Trixie and Bruce, 1936.

Mr and Mrs Ward, of Manor Farm, Nettleton, with their baby daughter, Eva, in 1916.

Mr Alfred Ward with his son, Alfred, and his grandson, Alfred, all of Manor Farm, Nettleton, 1931.

Albert Derrick outside the Jubilee Stores, Colerne, 1930s.

Mrs Amy Neate of Ford with her son William, 1912.

Mr Tom Neate (left) and his brother, William, at Tom's bungalow on the Bristol Road at Ford. Tom Neate was postman at Ford and serviced Post Office bicycles at Chippenham depot. The villages of Ford, Biddestone, Slaughterford and Castle Combe were included in his walking route.

Mrs Billett would buy chickens or ducklings from the market in Llanelli where her sister lived. She raised them to feed the family when they lived at Kent's Bottom at Yatton Keynell, just above Castle Combe.

Muriel Hulance outside her house, No. 8 Tiddleywink, Yatton Keynell, 1953. The original name of the area was Old Moorend. When Muriel was at school, the teacher told them that the name Tiddleywink derived from the time early in the century when the old village 'Bobby' would go into the pub that was there at the time and 'wink for his tiddley!'

Mrs Emma Grimshaw of Kellaways,
Chippenham, with her daughter, Alice, and
Betty Gainey outside Kellaways church, 1927.

Mrs Mary Anne Potter with her children outside their home at the mill house, Kellaways in
1906. Mabel (centre) was born in 1897,
Alfred (left) was born in 1898, Florence (right)
was born in 1901, and baby Annie was born
in 1904. In the bird cage to the right of the
door was a 'singing finch'. Keeping a finch
was a common practice in those days.

Mr William Anstee and his wife Rose, of Stanton St Quinton, thought to have been photographed on their wedding day in 1914. Mr Anstee worked as a general handyman, carrying out tasks such as hay cutting, hedge-laying, wood cutting and log selling. He came from Westbury-on-Trym, Bristol, married Rose from Hullavington, and settled in Stanton St Quinton. Mrs Anstee was laundress for several of the big houses in the area, Lady Margaret Spicer, the rector of Grittleton, and the Wilson family of Leigh Delamere among others. The laundry would be delivered to Mrs Anstee by the house chauffeurs.

Mr James Neal from Sherston with his wife, Elizabeth, in 1937. After their marriage they lived in Hullavington and had ten children. Mr Neal was a farm worker.

Mrs Annie Wicks with her daughters, Nellie, Dolly, Gladys, and Phyllis who is standing beside her mother. This photograph was taken just before the First World War.

Mr Robert Neal with his wife, Emma, and their four children, Hilda (Dolly), Joan, Violet and Stella, in 1916. This photograph was taken just before Robert went into the army in the First World War. Robert's home was in Hullavington until he and Emma married, when they settled in Corston.

Mr William Henry Pritchard with his wife, Rhoda, in the garden of their home in Noble Street, Sherston, 1920.

Lilian Pritchard with her fiancé, Edward Dore, on the occasion of their engagement, *c*. 1922. Lilian wore a pale blue dress. The locket she is wearing was a gift from her fiancé. They were married at Sherston parish church on 25 November 1922.

Mrs Harriett Pearce, widow of William Pearce, gamekeeper to Sir George Holford of Westonbirt, with her daughter Florence, who is holding her daughter, Edwina, outside Ivy Cottage, Cutwell, Tetbury in 1924.

Members of the Pritchard family at the home of Ted and Lilian Dore (neé Pritchard), who had the grocery shop in the High Street, Sherston, 1939. Back, left to right: Ted Dore, John Dore, Bill Pritchard, -?-, Emily Bloyce (neé Pritchard), Charlie Bloyce, Florence Pritchard. Front: Christine Arthand, Annette Arthand, Howard Bloyce, Mrs Dore senior, Christopher Dore, and Louie Arthand (neé Pritchard) with her youngest daughter, Pamela.

Sarah Smith, wife of Emmanuel, gamekeeper to Sir George Holford at Westonbirt House. Mr and Mrs Smith lived in the two lodges at the front gate of the house with their nine children, the last one born in 1851.

William Pritchard (1914), footman at Easton Grey House for Mr Thomas Smith, who was married to the aunt of Lady Violet Bonham-Carter.

Louisa Pritchard with her nephew, Peter, who died very soon after this picture was taken in 1920. He suffered from an intestinal imperfection which with today's technology could probably have been cured.

Dennis Pritchard with his grandson, John, having a tea break from working in the garden at Pinkney in the mid-1960s.

Mr Mark Poulton of Corston with his wife, Annie, and their children: Percy, who worked at Grittleton Stables, William, who became a butcher in Malmesbury, Charlie, who was killed in 1916 in the First World War, Harriet (Queenie), who worked at Lackham House near Lacock, and Emma.

The Webb family of Lea in 1939. Back row, left to right: Walter, Lil, Phyllis, Beattie, Winnie. Middle row: Flossie, Dorothy, Mr Mark Webb, Fred, Mrs Mary Webb, Ron. Front row: Norman, Ray, Elsie, Dolly, Gerald, Edna.

Emma Poulton from Corston worked at
Spye Park as still room maid.

This picture of Mr James A. Jones was
taken when he was mayor of
Malmesbury in 1910 and 1911. He held
the post several times after those dates
and is recognized as a great benefactor to
the town. In 1950 he became a Freeman
of Malmesbury and was re-elected as
alderman in his ninety-sixth year.

Mrs Harriet Pearce of Cutwell (centre) with, from the left, her son-in-law Albert Barret, his daughter Dorothy, Eva Pritchard, Letitia Barret, Florence Pritchard and Thomas Barret in 1922. They are pictured at the Fishponds bridge at Escourt Park, between Malmesbury and Tetbury.

Family gathering for Edwina Pritchard's second birthday, at Cutwell, Tetbury. From left to right: Lilian and Ted Dore, Eva Dore, Rhoda Pritchard, Alec Dore, Florence Pritchard (Edwina's mother) and Dennis Pritchard.

Clare, Countess of Cowley of Seagry House, wearing state robes for the coronation of King George V. She died tragically in a fire in around 1947, caused, it is thought, by a cigarette falling into her armchair. The house was badly damaged and the cook, Mrs Bradish, also died.

Mrs Ellen Couzens, wearing the sun bonnet, somewhere in her eighties, with Mr and Mrs Ferris. Mrs Couzens lived all her life in Draycott Cerne, and Mr and Mrs Ferris lived in Sutton Benger, where Mr Ferris worked on Manor Farm. This picture was taken in the early 1950s.

Mr and Mrs Bailey with their children, Frank and Evelyn, 1905. After her marriage to Edward Kite, Evelyn moved to Christian Malford, where she and her husband ran the General Store.

Mrs Edith Iles of Bradenstoke with her children. From the left: Lucy Annie, Ethel Ruth, Arthur Thomas George, baby Grace Louisa, Edith Mary and Florence Amy. This picture was taken during the First World War for their father, who served in France and Salonika with the Wiltshire Yeomanry.

# Churches and Weddings

Bertie Swan and Ellen Diana Preedy (known as Betty) after their wedding on 30 December 1933. They were married by the Revd Mr Appleford of Castle Combe and the Revd Mr Foster of Box, where Mr Swan was a schoolteacher. Betty carried a sheaf of lilies. Mr Swan's Best Man was Ken Addison, a friend of his brother Stanley who was killed in a motor cycle accident just before the wedding.

Mr and Mrs Joseph Swan with their daughters outside the Congregational chapel, Upper Combe on the occasion of their Diamond Wedding, 5 March 1950. Mr Swan was a lay preacher at the chapel. Standing, from the left: Nancy, Mr Swan, Floss, Mrs Swan, Win. Seated: Dorothy and Kathleen.

Fred Swan with his bride Elsie Taylor, 30 March 1957. They were married at Rodbourne parish church and settled in Castle Combe where Fred was a farm worker.

Gordon Swan of Castle Combe and his bride, Avril Ball of Lowden, had a guard of honour formed by Nettleton Cricket Club, and left the 'old' St Peter's church at Lowden under an arch of cricket bats on 20 March 1965. Fred Swan, brother of the groom, was Best Man and Sue Adams of Nettleton was bridesmaid. She wore a dress of pink. The King William public house, where she lived, closed some years ago and is now a private house. The guard of honour are, from the left: Paul Flint, Tony Daniels, Harold Crook, Ray Miles, Geoff Wilkins and Stan Chivers.

The wedding of Grace Eels and George Lugg, both of Castle Combe, *c.* 1935. Left to right: Elsie Stanley, Grace, George, Rita Eels and Sidney Lugg, the Best Man.

Alan Ward of Manor Farm, Nettleton and his bride, Dorothy Adams of Church Farm, West Kingston, a small, well hidden village to the west of Castle Combe. Alan and Dorothy were married at the Baptist chapel at Nettleton in the 1940s.

Ted Ward of Manor Farm, Nettleton and his bride, Rosemary Watkins, outside the Baptist chapel, Nettleton after their wedding in around 1947.

Biddestone parish church, dedicated to St Nicholas. There used to be a second church, dedicated to St Peter, but it was demolished in 1846.

The wedding at Biddestone of Joe Swan of Castle Combe and Alice Wright of Biddestone in 1913. Mr and Mrs Joseph Swan are on the left of the picture, and Fred Swan, Best Man is standing behind the groom.

The wedding of William Marsh of Yatton Keynell to Lavinia Golden of Bulkington, who lived at Green Farm, Nettleton, *c. 1925.* Jack Marsh, the groom's brother, was Best Man and is standing to the left of the picture with his mother and father, Mr and Mrs Charles Marsh, to his right.

Reginald Hulance and Muriel Beazer were married at Yatton Keynell Baptist chapel in 1953. Mr Cross from Bath officiated.

Doris Gainey, James Sage, Christina Gainey, William Gainey and his mother, Emma Gainey, after the wedding of James and Christina at Kington St Michael in 1956.

The Revd Mr Day served communion to his parishioners from a tomb when the church key holder went on holiday and forgot to leave behind the key of Stanton St Quinton church sometime around 1965. Left to right: Mrs Sheppard, Mrs Kingman, Mrs V. Cripps, Mr Burge, -?-, B. Starke, Miss Ella Turtle (housekeeper to Mr Day), -?-, Mrs Cripps, ? Hodgkinson, Mrs Hodgkinson, Angela Anstee.

Florence Potter and Walter Davey on their wedding day, in April 1926. Walter came from London to work with Mr Potter at Kellaways Mill. When the Second World War broke out Walter went to work at Westinghouse. They were married at Kellaways church and had two children, Philip and Barbara. Florence is carrying a sheaf of Arum lilies.

This picture of a meeting of the Strict Baptists, at Hullavington, was taken outside the Baptist chapel, in front of the bakery in Watts Lane, around 1908. Ada, wife of John Wicks, hurdle maker, is seated third from the right in the middle row; she has her son John on her lap. Her two older daughters are among the crowd of children, possibly those sitting at her feet. Mrs Alice Neal is seated farthest right.

Phyllis Wicks arriving at Hullavington church for her marriage to George Sterne in August 1934. The Revd G. Fabian Evans of Kington St Michael officiated as the village vicar was away. Miss Wicks wore an ivory silk dress, the gift of Mrs P. Du Cros of Allington Manor, where Phyllis worked. She carried a bouquet of pink carnations, which was placed on the War Memorial in memory of her brother who died in the First World War.

The wedding of Rose Wicks of Hullavington, and Charles Gale, of Grittleton, in April 1941. They are pictured outside their cottage in the Leys, Hullavington, where they lived until 1942, when they moved to Castle Combe, where their daughter Ros was born. Left to right: Dick Boulter (Best Man), Iris Gough, Charles Gale (groom), Rose Wicks (bride), Monica Boulter, Mr John Wicks (father of the bride), and Doris Dutton (best friend of the bride, from Draycott Cerne).

On the right hand side of this picture taken in the barnyard of Castle Barn Farm are the ivy-covered remains of the old castle at Badminton from which the farm takes its name. It shows the wedding of Harold Eddols to Lavinia Hughes on 14 September 1933, the Revd Mr Gibbs officiating, at Badminton church. Front row, left to right: Hilda Young, Harold Eddols, Lavinia Hughes, and Edith Hughes. Middle row: Mrs Pincott, Mr Hughes (bride's father), Mrs Lily Eddols (groom's mother), Mrs Nelly Hughes (bride's mother), Victor Hunter (Best Man) Maud Hughes, Rene ?. Back row: Ada Hughes, Sid Harris, Frederick Eddols (groom's father), Harry Bennett, Sarah Bennett, George Hughes.

Sherston Church Choir on the tower of the church of the Holy Cross. William Pritchard is standing third from the left. All six of the Pritchard children were choristers at the church as soon as they became old enough. This picture was taken around 1909.

The four daughters of Rhoda Pritchard at her graveside in the churchyard of Sherston parish church. She was fifty years old when she died of cancer on 6 June 1927. From the left: Emily (Bloyce), Eva (Dore), Lilian (Dore) and Louisa (Arthand).

Malmesbury Abbey from the back. A memorial garden now covers some of the land beneath the Abbey walls. It was opened by Her Royal Highness Princess Anne in May 1980 and is called the Cloister Garden.

Jack Bishop and Olive Jones were married at Malmesbury Abbey on 6 June 1938. Olive was Akela for the 1st Malmesbury Cubs at the time and a Guider herself, hence the guard of honour of Guides, Scouts, Cubs and Rover Scouts. She was also a teacher at the Abbey Sunday School and the vicar, the Revd Mr Dean, interrupted his holiday to officiate at her wedding. On the left is the Brown Owl of the Brownie Pack, Doctor Moore's wife is on the right, Roy Madge was Best Man, and Beryl Greenfield was bridesmaid.

The Christmas story being acted out by the Sunday School of Malmesbury Abbey in around 1938. Muriel Jones took the part of Mary, and Joseph was played by the curate of St Mary's church, Malmesbury.

George Shingles was the gas-lamp lighter in Malmesbury. Here we see him with his bride, Lilly Webb, in 1948. Left to right: Jean Webb, Dick Shingles, Elsie Webb, George and Lilly, Mr Mark Webb, Julie Carey and Edna Webb.

The wedding of Mr and Mrs Alan Baker at Lea church, *c.* 1948. Mr Howard Baker is beside the groom, and beside the bride is her father, Mr Mark Webb. The bridesmaids, Ruth and Maureen Baker, were sisters of the groom.

The wedding of Mr and Mrs Joe Nash, whose reception was held in Lea Memorial Hall, around 1950.

The wedding of Blanche Thomas and Arthur Couzens, at Draycott Cerne church, in July 1932. Draycott Cerne church is very small and no longer used. It is about 700 years old, has a fifteenth-century porch, three windows and three sundials. It is also one of the few Wiltshire churches with a fireplace. On the floor are brass portraits of Sir Edward Cerne and his lady. Sir Thomas Long married into the Cerne family in Tudor times, and the Long family monuments run through the seventeenth and eighteenth centuries. The estate then came into the hands of the Cowley family, and the marble bust of Adelaide, the eight-year-old daughter of Lord and Lady Cowley born about 150 years ago, was placed in the church on her death.

The Revd Mr Fellowes, vicar of Draycott Cerne from 1880 to 1890, was such a handsome chap that all the ladies from the villages around would walk their daughters to his church to try and catch his eye. Clever man, he escaped and moved on to another parish.

Little Somerford Church.

Little Somerford church, described by John Betjeman as 'worth cycling twelve miles against the wind to see', has stood for over 700 years and has many unusual and distinctive features, such as the fifteenth-century porch with scratch sundial and a two-tier pulpit of Jacobean construction.

A family group outside Poplar Farm after the wedding of Francis (Frank) Charles Dee to Mamie Lea at Sutton Benger parish church in the early 1920s. Mr and Mrs Lea of Poplar Farm are on the left of the picture, and Mr and Mrs Dee of Great Somerford on the right.

The wedding of Edward and Evelyn Kite at Littleton Panell Wesleyan church in 1929. Evelyn is wearing an unusual short wedding gown and carrying a bouquet of red roses. Left to right: Albert Kite, Emily Kite, Frank Bailey, Marjorie Kite, Edward and Evelyn, Hilda Gaisford, Annie Bailey and Frank John Bailey. After their wedding they lived in Christian Malford, where they ran a grocery shop and Edward practised his craft as a cordwainer, a little used word which describes a shoemaker.

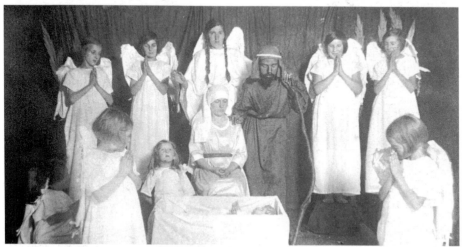

Sutton Benger Sunday School performing the Nativity, 1933. The angels are, left to right: Lilian Hawkins, -?-, Olive Ball, -?-, Miss Hayter (sister of the rector), Margery Gardener, Rachel Parsons (?), Gwen Walker. Mary was played by Mary Bond, Joseph by Dick Smith, and the cherub beside Mary was Betty Walker.

J.BARRINGTON. L.HUMPHRIES.
S.COUSENS. R.LEA.
C.COLE. A.LEWIS.
J.HEATH. H.PARSONS.

WHO GAVE THEIR LIVES FOR KING AND COUNTRY

This beautifully carved war memorial was erected within the churchyard of All Saints' at Sutton Benger. It commemorates those who gave their lives in the First World War.

# SECTION FIVE

# Occupations

Mr Seymour Eels, of Eastcombe Farm, Castle Combe, standing sheaves of corn to make a stook, 1930. These can be seen in the back of the picture. After reaping, the crop would be bound into bundles or sheaves which were then leant against each other to dry.

Mrs Ann Granger standing to the left of the doorway of her grocery shop near the Market Place at Castle Combe, 1895. The sign over the door reads, 'Ann Granger, Dealer in Tea, Coffee and Provisions, Licensed to sell Tobacco.' The frame to the right of the door has a selection of views of Castle Combe and the window is filled with large jars of sweets.

Perhaps the ultimate in village occupations! Castle Combe itself was the star of *Dr Dolittle* in 1971. The trout stream was dammed and other minor cosmetic changes made to make the streamside houses look like the harbour of a fishing village.

Robin, the horse which drew the milk cart around Castle Combe for at least fourteen years and knew the round perfectly. Holding Robin in 1930 is Mr John Eels, with Mr Albert Eels standing in the doorway behind them. Albert Eels' grandsons still run the business, now called the Chippenham and Castle Combe Dairies, from the same premises in Castle Combe.

Castle Combe Dairy, originally a family concern owned by Mr and Mrs Eels of Castle Combe, now has a large depot in Chippenham.

Mr William Marsh, standing in Nettleton road with Miss Ward, John King and Denis Marsh in the mid-1950s. (The other seated persons are not known.) Mr Raymond King is holding Duke the horse.

Mr Dick Tarling in the late 1930s with Silver, the last horse to work at Manor Farm, Nettleton. The steps lead up to the hayloft over the barn, and the little archway beneath was a kennel intended for the use of a farm dog but never used, as the farm dogs were pets.

The staff of the White Hart Inn at Ford pictured outside the inn in 1938. Leon Arthand, who lived in Chapel Lane, now called the Old Coach Road, is second from the right.

Members of the road gang employed by Wiltshire County Council for the maintenance of roads in the Ford area. The big, heavy steamroller was a familiar sight in those days. Left to right: Arthur Hunt, Tom Wright, Buller Hayward, -?-, -?-, Mr Burgess, Fred Rawlings, Harry Moore, -?-, -?-, -?-, -?-, -?-, Tom Jaques.

This is thought to show Orchard Sawmills at Biddestone, sited between the two public houses in the centre of the village. The bearded gentleman seated on the right is thought by the oldest resident in Yatton Keynell to be the carter for Orchards. The picture dates from around 1910.

Mr William Smith, horse dealer of Yatton Keynell, completing a transaction in Wales in June 1947. Evan, from whom he had bought the horses, is standing to the right.

Mr Jim Hulance, far left, in the late 1920s, with horses from Foscott on the Grittleton Estate, where Mr Hulance worked for Sir Audley Neeld.

Edwin Northover PC 175. On completion of his training at Devizes he moved to Swindon, then to Bradford-on-Avon where his daughters were born. Throughout the Second World War he was at Grittleton, and in 1949/50 he moved to Lacock where he stayed until he retired.

Mrs Gertrude Webb at Willow Barn, Kington Langley. Mr William Webb worked at Middle Farm for thirty-seven years. When clearing snow at Bencroft, between Stanley and Bremhill, in 1945, Mr Webb and his crew found a rabbit in a tree where it had taken refuge because the snow was so deep.

Neddy the donkey with his owner Mr Jim Wicks, hurdle maker of Hullavington, standing outside his shelter in Stanton Woods. Lady Avice Spicer, his employer, had the photograph taken during the 1930s to show Mr Wicks working at his craft.

Tree felling at Willesley near Sherston. Sadly, none of these gentlemen's names are known. It is thought the photograph may have been taken by a member of the family of Mr Pearce, gamekeeper to Sir George Holford, at Westonbirt House in the 1920s.

Mrs Lilian Dore with her son Christopher James and Sister Lewis, the village midwife who delivered him. Mrs Dore and her husband Edward (Ted) had a grocery shop in the High Street, Sherston. This picture was taken in their back garden in 1936.

William Pritchard helping on his father's
smallholding at Sherston, 1911.

Lilian and Edward Dore with Ted's mother, Elizabeth, outside the door of their grocery
shop in the High Street, Sherston, 1922–3. Puritan Soap and Oxo are advertised on the
windows and an ornate oil lamp hangs in the centre.

William Pritchard, of Tetbury, mowing the cricket pitch at Westonbirt House, the home of Sir George Holford, *c.* 1920. The mowing machine was invented by Edwin Budding of Stroud, who signed an agreement with John Ferrabee of the Phoenix Works, Thrupp, near Stroud for his machinery to be manufactured there. This iron works is now the home of Alan Sutton Publishing. Budding's mowing machine was described as heavy and inefficiently geared. A large machine cost ten guineas and a small one seven guineas in 1831, the first recorded customer being the head gardener at Regent's Park Zoo.

Mr William Norris, of Lewis Lane, Cirencester, painting the sign for the Hare and Hounds Hotel, Westonbirt, 1969. This sign is still in position at the hotel. William trained in London as a pictorial sign maker and sign writer.

Mr Emmanuel Smith with his wife Sarah (neé Tandy, of Sherston), *c.* 1855. Mr Smith was gamekeeper for Sir George Holford and later his son, Robert Holford of Westonbirt. With them is their son William.

Jones and Son, Cycle Repairers of Malmesbury, on 18 December 1913. Charles White, first left, started his own business just before the First World War. On his return from active service he extended his business to motor cycles and is still in business today. Bill Clark, from Abbey Mill, is second left.

Mr Harold Jones, of Aberavon in Wales, came to Malmesbury in 1930 to build the surviving Cowbridge, in Cowbridge Road, near Sir Philip Henlocke's house. Ernest Ireland was the contractor; Mr Jones was in charge of the engineering. Cowbridge Road had to be widened for the bridge to be built. Mr Jones and his family settled in Malmesbury after this particular contract was completed.

Girls from the E.K. Cole (EKCO) assembly lines, Cowbridge, Malmesbury take a break from building radar equipment during the Second World War. Among those pictured are May Eldridge, Mary Warner and Eve Giles, standing first, third and fourth from the left in the back row.

Mrs Lizzie Barnes and her daughter Dorothy with samples of lace they have made. Mrs Barnes was one of the pupils of Lady Suffolk's Lace School, which was set up in the Market Room of the King's Arms Hotel in Malmesbury High Street in 1907. Dorothy was taught the craft by her mother.

Mr Joseph Barnes, carpenter and coffin maker, in his workshop in the High Street, Malmesbury. Mr Barnes was born in 1846.

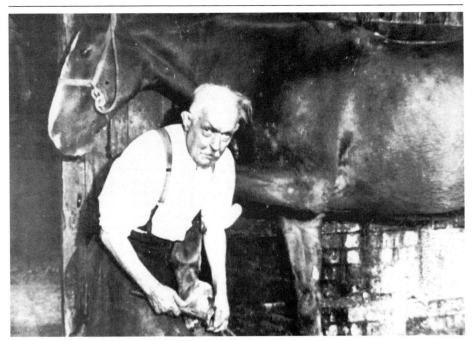

George Gregory, blacksmith of Great Somerford, shoeing Tangy in the mid-1940s.

Bill Couzens, of Draycott Cerne, with his horse, Trigger, which he used for carting and farming jobs around the villages. Mr Couzens died in 1919.

Sutton Benger Garage, which was started by Frank Dee in the barn of Poplar Farm in around 1922. The wooden building to the right of the picture was the Forge; it burnt down in the mid-1930s! On the side of the lorry is an advertising banner for 'Deering Harvester Service', for whom Mr Dee was agent. Deering's name is also on the Forge and either side of the barn door. Mobiloil was dispensed from the tanks on the right, Shell Oil from that on the second right, and Texaco petrol is advertised on two lights above the petrol pumps.

Bob Poole and Dennis Matthews with his daughter Sandra on the Ferguson tractor which was used to pull 'Fred' the plough at Lower Seagry Farm.

Herb collecting was a community task, as can be seen from this photograph of children from around Sutton Benger taken during the First World War. Outside Sutton Benger the old shed that was used for drying the herbs once they had been gathered still stands. Blanche Thomas, centre back, wearing the large Panama hat, moved to Draycott Cerne at the age of two years. She married Arthur Couzens of Stanton St Quinton in 1932. They had one son, Reuben, who still lives in Draycott Cerne today. Blanche died at the age of 81 years.

Mr George Hawkins, builder of Sutton Benger, working with his team to repair a dry stone wall around the house called The Starlings. This picture was taken in the late 1940s.

Mr Albert Kite, father of Edward, owner of the village General Store in Christian Malford, with his grandson Clive, Edward's eldest son, in 1933. Mr Kite is standing beside the shop outbuildings; behind him is the stable door. In the background is the workshop of Mr Granger, who was a builder and handyman.

Mollie Hughes, of Avonweir Nurseries, harrowing the land ready for a crop of vegetables to be sown during the Second World War. Her pony Terry is being used to pull the harrow.

# Transport

Mr Charles Gough of School Lane, Grittleton, head carter for Sir Audley Neeld on the Grittleton Estate. Mr Gough was sexton at Grittleton church and Bell Captain, and was often to be seen riding around the villages on his tricycle. This picture was taken around his seventieth birthday.

Mr Jack Marsh, in his Model T Ford, outside Green Farm, Nettleton. The pond was lawned over soon after this picture was taken some time in the late 1920s. The car's registration number is V2387.

Mr William Marsh, of Green Farm, Nettleton, in his Jowett automobile, May 1930.

Mr Jim Wicks, hurdle maker of Hullavington, with John Tyler of Chippenham, in his cart drawn by the donkey Neddy, *c.* 1930. John was related to the Wicks family and often went to visit them.

Mrs Phyllis Stern in the driving seat of this motor cycle combination in the lane at Newtown, Hullavington, *c.* 1929. Behind her on the bike is her niece Marion Fry, and in the sidecar are her sister Enid Wicks and her brother Jim.

Hullavington railway station in the early 1930s, one of the stations closed by Dr Beeching. Passenger traffic ceased in 1951, and the goods yard closed in 1962.

Mr George Sterne, at the age of 17 years, was employed at Hullavington station and is shown here pushing a trolley on the station platform, with a workmate, probably Harry Peters, in 1929. When Mr Sterne was on his way to work at Great Somerford station on 18 April 1949, an airman fell from the platform at Dauntsey station into the path of the train on which Mr Sterne was travelling. He went straight to the airman's assistance and, according to the newspaper report, his prompt action was the only thing that saved the airman's life, his arm having been severed. Mr Sterne was awarded for his bravery and had to go to London for the presentation.

Emily (née Pritchard) and Charles Bloyce in an already somewhat outdated Model T Ford after their wedding at Sherston parish church in 1920. These cars were assembled in Manchester and sold for around £132. This model would have had the two-speed controlled transmission, but by 1921 the Model T featured a three-speed sliding type gearbox.

Edward Dore in his very adaptable Model T Ford, *c.* 1920. Here it is in use as a delivery lorry. He also used it as a taxi, with its alternative bodywork in place. An advertisement offering this car for hire is seen in the shop window.

Eva Dore, wearing the leather driving helmet she always wore when riding pillion, on her husband's motor cycle combination, in 1933.

Alec Dore in his 1934 Morris Minor 8 Series car, with his daughter Margaret just discernible in the front passenger seat.

Jones and Sons' cycle shop (now Knee's Furnishers) in the High Street, Malmesbury. They were open until 10 p.m. most evenings, and Jimmy Jones had one of the first cars in the town. Judging by the cars in front of the shop window, this picture was taken in around 1910. We think it shows two 1910 Model T Fords and a Valveless 25hp in the centre.

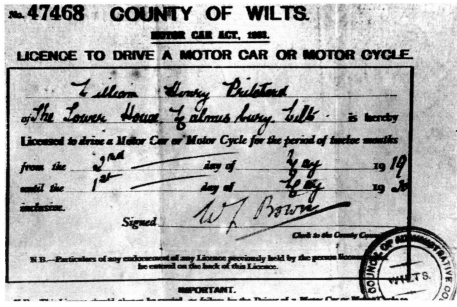

The driving licence of William Pritchard, who was employed as chauffeur to a doctor who lived at Tower House, Malmesbury. William learned to drive while serving in the army during the First World War. A driving licence could be replaced at the cost of one shilling, and renewed annually at the cost of five shillings. A fine not exceeding five pounds could be imposed if the licence could not be produced on demand by a police constable. The date of this licence is 2 May 1919.

This Lincoln Imp engine was manufactured by Ruston Proctor and operated by Dick Bishop and George Vanstone at the old Cinema, owned by Mr Jack Mall. The Cinema was a wooden hut in the High Street at Malmesbury. Dorothy Barnes, who lived next door, is sitting on the machine in around 1930.

Malmesbury railway station, with a very clear view of the Abbey.

Tetbury Great Western Railway station in the early 1930s. This station closed on 4 April 1964.

Some of those who gathered to see the departure of the last train from Tetbury station. Bob Gregg, holding the wreath, and Fred Hills, far right, helped to mark the passing of this service on 4 April 1964.

Mrs Harriet Pearce, at the wheel of her son's Model T Ford, outside her cottage at Cutwell in Tetbury in the early 1920s.

William Pritchard in his Morris Minor at Cutwell, Tetbury. The car had an 847 cc engine and cost approximately £100 in 1934. Note the forward-opening windscreen. The car was dark green in colour.

Dr Forbes Fraser, grandfather of Mollie Hughes of Avonweir, Christian Malford, outside his consulting rooms at the Circus in Bath, seated in what we think is a Victorian style phaeton.

Mr Thomas McGivern with the milk float and mare, June, that belonged to Mr R.C. Tucker, of Summerlands Farm, Christian Malford, *c.* 1945.

# SECTION SEVEN
# Wartime

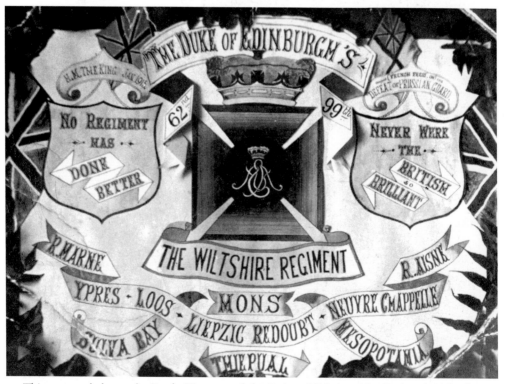

This postcard shows the Battle Honours of the Duke of Edinburgh's 62nd and 99th, the Wiltshire Regiment. It was sent by William Pritchard to his family while he was convalescing after the First World War, on 12 March 1919. Bill served with the 3rd Battalion, the Wiltshire Regiment. He enlisted on 10 May 1916, was sent to France on 31 September 1916, injured on 10 March 1917, reported back to the 3rd Battalion on 26 June 1917, classified C111, and continued so until discharge when he returned to his home in Tetbury.

Guns of the Wiltshire Regiment in action in Egypt during the First World War. This photograph was taken by Bill Pritchard while he was serving there.

Roland Alphaus Pullen, of Castle Combe, worked as a gardener at the Manor. The young men of the village were given no choice about 'signing on' at the outbreak of war in 1914: they were told there was no work for them. So he and his brother Bert enlisted into the Gloucestershire Regiment and went to France. There Roland was shot and was brought back to England by ambulance train. He died in Guys Hospital at the age of nineteen. He was one of the eight from Castle Combe who died in the First World War. Roland is the only one of these buried in the village churchyard as he was the only one to die in England. His grave is marked by a military headstone.

This delightful photograph is thought to be of nursing friends of Nancy Swan of Castle Combe, who had been an army nurse for a period during the First World War. It is dated 1917 and has the message, 'Sincerely Yours, Hilda.'

Jack Macey, uncle of Albert Derrick of Colerne. This photograph was taken on 11 August 1900, before Jack left to take part in the South African Campaign. He died in South Africa, of enteric fever.

Her Majesty Queen Mary with New Zealand lumberjacks who were billeted at Grittleton towards the end of the Second World War, 1945. The men were employed in felling trees at Grittleton, Bowood and Longleat.

Police Constable 'Bunny' Northover, who was stationed at Grittleton and then Lacock, holding one of the incendiary bombs that fell on his 'patch' during the Second World War.

Arthur Couzens of Stanton St Quinton, who was a security guard at Hullavington Aerodrome during the Second World War.

Joyce Donnison, corporal in charge of the station post office at Hullavington Royal Air Force Station where she served for five years, in 1958. Joyce married locally and maintained close contact with the station until its closure in 1992.

This plaque was presented to Joyce on the occasion of her sixty-second birthday. Hullavington Station closed the next year. Owing to ill health, Joyce was unable to attend the closing ceremony to which she had been invited.

The hangars being built at Hullavington Aerodrome at the outbreak of the Second World War, 1939. One of these hangars was the victim of an arson attack, by two airmen serving on the station, in 1991. Hullavington closed as a military air base in 1992.

Some of the men employed on the construction of the aerodrome at Hullavington, at the outbreak of the Second World War.

Mr John Wicks and his wife Ada Jane, of Hullavington, pictured before John left for action in the First World War, from which he came home safely. John and Ada had eight children, John, Maurice, Frank, Lilian, Mary, Cecily and Rose. One baby died.

Jack Giles of Bromham at the outbreak of the First World War. He served in the field artillery. He survived the war, and moved to Manor Farm, Hullavington, around 1936.

Harry Pearce of Westonbirt and his wife Amy just before the outbreak of the First World War. Harry was employed as chauffeur to Mr Fyffe, of Fyffe's Bananas, at Box near Minchinhampton.

William Henry Pritchard, born at Pinkney, later of Sherston, dressed in uniform for the South Africa Campaign, 1900.

Colin Bishop of Malmesbury was killed in France at the age of seventeen. His parents received this undated stereotyped message from Buckingham Palace. It is signed by King George V.

George Baker left school at the age of nine to work with horses in Cirencester. His home had been at Chipping Steps, Malmesbury. He was married on 18 March 1913. His daughter Eunice was christened on the day the First World War was declared, 1 August 1914, and George went into the army almost from the beginning, at the age of eighteen. He served with the Royal Field Artillery, still working with horses. He is shown here mounted on the smaller of the two. His daughter believes the photograph was taken at Gallipoli. George survived the war and lived to the age of eighty.

Ronald and Walter Webb, of Lea, on leave together in 1940. Walter was killed in France in 1944.

The grave of Walter Webb of Lea, who was killed in action. Walter was a sergeant in the Wiltshire Regiment.

Joseph Baker, of Tetbury, joined the Royal Air Force at the age of seventeen before the outbreak of the Second World War. This photograph shows him, second from the right in the front row, on completion of his training at Yatesbury. Joseph served as gunner on the bomber aeroplanes during the war. He served in many places around the world and was shot down when his plane was returning to Colombo from Singapore.

William Pritchard, of Tetbury, stands to the right of this party of fitters at Kemble Airfield. Spitfire MK1X MK997 was made by Vickers Armstrong at Castle Bromwich in 1944 and allocated to No. 1 Squadron on 16 April. It was damaged on 5 July at Detling, Kent, probably countering the V1 menace. This picture was taken in March or April 1948, just prior to the plane's export to Norway, where it probably flew with 332 Squadron at Gardermoen, near Oslo. It is no longer flying, and is presumed to have been scrapped in Norway. We are indebted to Mr Anthony White, Assistant Archivist for the Spitfire Society, for this information.

Having completed their initial training course, these boys are about to leave for First World War France, on 31 September 1916. William Pritchard is standing in the centre of the back row.

The bridge at Draycott Cerne, photographed from Draycott House, weakened by army jeeps and other vehicles driven by American troops billeted there during the Second World War. When they left they gave money towards the cost of a new bridge.

Robert Gainey of Langley Burrell with his wife, Alice, and their son, Douglas. Bob served in the Somerset Light Infantry, and after his discharge from the army the family lived in Taunton.

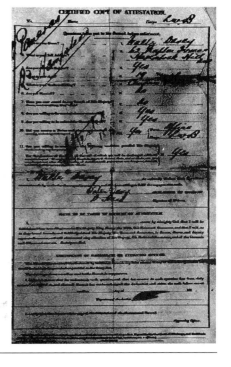

A copy of the Certificate of Attestation signed by recruits before enlisting into the army during the First World War. This one is signed by Walter Davey, in London. He was aged 19 years and 3 months and his occupation was Canvas Preparer. It is dated 9 December 1915. Walter survived the war and married Florence, the daughter of Mr Potter, miller of Kellaways.

# SECTION EIGHT
# Occasions

Mary Beazer presented this bouquet to Lady Wood of Longstone, Yatton Keynell, when she opened the original village hall in 1949.

The peace celebrations in Grittleton Park, the home of Sir Audley Neeld, in 1919. This picture was sent on a postcard from Mrs Billet, of Grittleton, to her niece at Caudle Green, near Cirencester. Standing, centre back, is Mr Amos, the headmaster of the village school. The message on the back of the card reads, 'I am mark on hat [fourth from left under second banner]. Alfred is in second row with a cap on [first on left in first standing row]. G. 'as a white hat on and Fred is at the end with a flag with a 0 on his chest [third row back, first left; the 0 appears to be a medallion]. Betty is at the other end, she's got your hat on [second from end of third row on the right].'

The children of Grittleton Village School, with their teachers and mothers, on an outing to Gough's Caves, Cheddar in 1923–4. Mrs Billett is standing behind the driver, holding her daughter Grace; three more of her children are sitting in the coach which was hired from Sudweeks Coaches of Devizes.

Staff of Sir Audley Neeld, of Grittleton Hall, setting out for the Alderton Races, 1929–30. Sir Audley supplied the transport and gave his staff the day off for the occasion. The small child being held up near the horse is Sir Audley's great niece.

Grittleton's 1945 victory celebrations included a fancy dress cricket match. Police Constable 'Bunny' Northover (called 'Bunny' because he could wiggle his nose!) played his part in the fun by dressing in a bathing suit and a topper.

Hullavington Church Choir on their annual outing, *c.* 1935. The Revd Mr Mortimer is standing beside the charabanc in the trilby hat, Mrs Phyllis Stern is seated third from right in the bus, and Mrs Nelly Bugden is fifth from the right.

Her Majesty Queen Elizabeth II with the Duke of Edinburgh and the late Duke and Duchess of Beaufort at the Badminton Horse Trials, 1961.

Her Majesty Queen Mary on one of her many visits to Malmesbury Abbey. She frequently stayed at Badminton House, with the Duke and Duchess of Beaufort, and loved to attend the service at the Abbey whenever possible. She also visited Westonbirt House, the home of Sir George Holford who was Extra Equerry to His Majesty King George V. Sir George can be seen beside the car, waiting for the Queen to enter it. He died in 1926.

The Old Court Room, Malmesbury. On the wall behind the Alderman's Chair is the royal coat of arms of William and Mary, dated 1693, flanked by the arms of the Earle family, who lived at Hankerton, and of John Cromwell, Burgess of Malmesbury. The Court Room is one of Malmesbury's medieval buildings. The earliest Minute book is dated 1600. There are five maces in the Old Corporation insignia, though usually, as in this picture, only four are seen.

Diamond + Jubilee + Celebration,
22nd June, 1897.

CHILDREN'S FETE,
MALMESBURY.
1837 ~ 1897

This invitation to a children's fête was one of many sent to the children of Malmesbury to celebrate the Diamond Jubilee of Her Majesty Queen Victoria on 22 June 1897.

A new commoner being sworn in on Malmesbury Common, January 1924. This ceremony dates back to at least the time of King Athelstone (924–39) for, according to the booklet published by the Friends of Malmesbury Abbey entitled *A History of Malmesbury* each new commoner is dealt three blows on the back with a branch and the following words are recited: 'This turf and twig I give to thee, As free as Athelstone gave to me, And I hope a loving brother thou wilt be.' From the left: Ambrose Clark, Mr Exton, Mr Box and James Pike.

Lea WI's entry in the Malmesbury Carnival during the 1950s was their 'Wedgwood Display'. Dorothy Hutton is on the left and Edna Parsons on the far right in this clever representation of Wedgwood motifs.

Tetbury Cenotaph, shrouded in the Union flag, before the ceremony of dedication at St Saviour's church (known in the town as the 'new church') just after the First World War.

*Chippenham*

*Mr & Mrs Matthews*
*Lower Seagry Farm*

*Congratulations for Your*
*25 Wedding Anniversary*
*from*
*Auntie Lil & Uncle Ern*

Telegrams were a speedy way of sending greetings until October 1982. Birthdays, weddings, births and deaths were all once marked in this way in most families, as telephones were not in such general use as today. This telegram was sent to Mr and Mrs Denis Matthews, of Lower Seagry Farm, on the occasion of their twenty-fifth wedding anniversary, 15 November 1966.

Countess Cowley, in the centre of the picture, and her daughters Lady Cecelia, with her dog Vim-Boy, and Lady Diana and husband. Lady Cowley's home was at Seagry House, Upper Seagry.

Grittleton Girl Guides outside the rectory in 1928, thought to be celebrating Empire Day which was held on 24 May, Queen Victoria's birthday. Front row, left to right: Joan Smith, Christine Hulance, Lily Knot, Lily Gainey, Bessie Billett. Middle row: Florence Wheeler, Miss Rudler, Lieutenant Miss Gowering, Captain Doris Holborrow (daughter of the rector of Grittleton), Eva Knott. Back row: Ethel Gray, Kathleen Haines (holding the banner), Peggy Harding, Daisy Lye, Roma Gray (with the Union flag).

A tea party, given for the elderly folk of Sutton Benger, at the village hall, some time in the 1960s.

Mr Sid Hillier, who drove the baker's cart in Christian Malford, dressed, it is thought, for the celebration of the end of the Second World War.

Sutton Benger Women's Institute holding their meeting in the garden of a cottage near Draycott Cerne church in the late 1950s.

# Sport and Leisure

Two daring young ladies in 1920, not only wearing bathing dresses but daring to be photographed in them! Louisa Pritchard is sitting on the stool and her sister Eva on the floor. Both girls came from Sherston.

Strolling through Longdean, between Castle Combe and Ford, is a most relaxing pastime for a summer afternoon, as long as you obey the notice on the gate and 'Beware of Snakes'! This was taken some time in the 1940s.

Nettleton Cricket Club, probably photographed at Nettleton in the late 1950s. Back row, left to right: Gordon Swan, Roy Wright, Paul Flint and Ivor Hayward. Seated, front: Peter Long(?) and Geoff Wilkins.

Albert Derrick of Colerne, with Ted, Eva and Jack Ward of Manor Farm, Nettleton, in 1935. Albert would visit the farm on the pretence of going shooting but really to court Eva. He would cycle from Colerne, a journey of approximately five miles.

A badger hunt somewhere in the Ford–Castle Combe valley in the 1920s. A dead badger is held up as a trophy on either side of these 'huntsmen'. They were considered quite social occasions, so the ladies sitting in the car were probably there as observers and to supply refreshment to the hunters after their hard work! Bill Neate of Ford is seated on the left of the front row with his dog Tiger.

His Grace the Duke of Beaufort, with Captain Frank Spicer to his left, judging a 'private driven' class at Grittleton Horse Show towards the end of the Second World War. The judges are just passing the vehicle of Lady Cooper of Chippenham. Behind them, almost hidden by the gentleman between them, is Miss Hussey of The Beeches, Great Somerford.

Children in costume for a play at Grittleton School, 1924–5. It may have been *Puss in Boots*. Among those whose names are known are, front row: Ethel Gray, Maggie Gilham, Eva Knott, Roma Gray. Second row: Florence Wheeler, Betty Archard, Bob Hopkins, Joan Smith, Phyllis Kington, Bessie Billet. Standing at the back: Jim Smith, Stanley Holborrow, Frank Avenell, Lesley Fry, Kathleen Haines (the witch), Cora Moore, Christine Hulance, Gwen Coleman, Jim Coleman, Roy Mann.

Pony rides at Dauntsey House during a Conservative fête in the mid-1940s.

Anne Draper, daughter of the miller of Kellaways Mill, John Potter, in the lane outside the mill with her 'sit-up-and-beg' bicycle in 1922.

Mr John Potter, miller of Kellaways, standing in the doorway of the mill with neighbour Mr Curtis, holding what appears to be a large eel, at some time in the 1940s.

Ivy Few, of Manor Farm, Hullavington, was the youngest of fourteen children. All six of her brothers and one sister, Daisy, went to America to live with an uncle in Ohio, having left school at the age of 14. Ivy is mounted on Tilley, a horse that she entered in many gymkhanas, in around 1908.

Hullavington First Eleven football team at the Grittleton victory celebrations in 1945.

The hounds of the Beaufort Hunt wait to set off at a meet at Worcester Lodge, Badminton Park in the 1940s. A timeless picture. The only things that change are the fashions worn by the spectators and followers of the hunt.

Mr Henry Pritchard of Sherston at Weston-Super-Mare in 1962. With him are his son William and great grandsons Tony and Roger, who all lived in Tetbury.

Alec Dore, with his daughter Margaret, on a family picnic at Sherston Cliffs, 1937. Beside Margaret is her cousin Annette, her aunt Louisa Arthand, mother Eva and cousin Christine. Alec would drive the female members of the family on these outings, and Louisa's husband Leon would ride his BSA motor cycle as there wasn't room for him in the car. The capacity was further reduced some months later, when his youngest daughter Pamela was born.

Ted Reed, huntsman with the Beaufort Hunt, leading his hounds away at Bingham Woods, near Rodbourne, past a group of motor cars belonging to followers of the hunt, in the mid-1940s.

First Malmesbury Ranger Guides, 1935. The Leader, Olive Jones, is standing first left in the back row; beside her is Muriel Jones, then Joan Clark, but the fourth girl's name is unknown. In the middle is Edna Lucas. In the front row, from the left, are Madge Hurst, ? Alexander, Betty Clark, and another unknown guide.

Mrs Marjorie Webb, of Winkworth
Cottage, Lea, pictured enjoying the
snows of 1930. Mrs Webb had a total
of fifteen children, so there was plenty
of demand on her time to play.

Amateur dramatics performed at
Malmesbury Town Hall, 1929. Olive
Jones was the Fairy Queen; Bessy Phillips,
standing, and Tansy Lane, sitting at
Olive's feet, were her attendants.

Edwina Pritchard stopping for refreshment in the middle of a cycle ride from her home in Cutwell, Tetbury to Cirencester during the Second World War. Note the thatched hayrick behind her.

John Cooper and his wife Sarah. Mr Cooper was overseer at Cook's Brewery, Hampton Street, Tetbury, where a Mr Woodward was manager in around 1910. Mr and Mrs Cooper moved from Sherston to Coombes Mead, now called London Road. He was organist at the Wesleyan chapel in Hampton Street. The chapel was situated behind a cottage and access was by means of a passage at the side of a house occupied by Mr Fry, the postman, at that time. The chapel has since been demolished and retirement homes built in its place.

The pantomime *Aladdin*, performed at Bremilham School by the Somerford Showtime Dancers trained by Mrs Christine Colman. From left to right: -?-, Karen Porter, Lorraine Heel, Susan Pelham, Sandra Matthews, -?-, Debbie ?, Kay Fitzcharles, Biddy Ryan, Celia Vincent, Debbie Frayling, Diane Hicks, -?-, -?-, Julie ?, Debbie Fletcher.

Earthstoppers for the Beaufort Hunt, gathered at the Wellesley Arms, Sutton Benger, 1921. Tom Newman, huntsman, is standing to the left of seated group who are Ben Fry, keeper at Stanton Park, Sid Hillier, of Christian Malford, 'The Master', when he was still the Marquis of Worcester (the late Duke of Beaufort), and Ben Hunt, keeper at Birds Marsh.

Rosemary Jones, of Kington Langley, on Rhumba, and Mollie Hughes, of Christian Malford, on Terry, taking part in the 'Gretna Green' race at the Wootton Bassett Horse Show, 1947.

Kenny Fry, of Summerlands Farm, and his sister Hazel, in the foreground, dressed as gipsies with their 'Gipsy Caravan' (a small pony tub in disguise!), ready to enter the fancy dress section of a horse show at Christian Malford during the Second World War, when fund raising was an important part of the war effort.

Mrs Barkwell, wife of Canon Barkwell of Christian Malford, leading her daughter Joan, Mr Lean of Bradenstoke and Heather Nightingale of Christian Malford, at Foxham, during the mid-1940s.

The Beaufort Hunt meeting at the Mermaid Inn, Christian Malford in the mid-1940s. Bert Pateman is on the left and Ted Reed, huntsman, on the right.

An unknown fisherman proudly displaying his catch, a large pike taken from the River Avon at Avonweir Nurseries, Christian Malford, in the late 1930s.

The Beaufort Hunt about to set off from The Jolly Trooper public house at Bradenstoke on 8 February 1951.

Castle Combe's beauty is internationally renowned, as is shown by this picture taken in the 1970s of Dorothy Higgs just outside Durban, South Africa, where an architect was attempting to recreate the village that so inspired him. Dorothy assured us that the copy was nowhere near as beautiful as the original, as we can see!

# *Acknowledgements*

Mr and Mrs Anstee • Miss D. Barnes • Mrs O. Bishop • Mr and Mrs H. Bloyce
Mrs E. Brown • Mr and Mrs R. Couzens • Mrs E. Dagger • Mr J. Dee
Mrs E. Derrick • Mr C. Dore • Mr and Mrs J. Dore • Mrs B. Drew
Mrs L. Eddols • Mrs L. Emmett • Mrs P. Faulkner • Mr and Mrs C. Gale
Mrs Hazel • Mrs J. Hughes • Mrs R. Hulance • Mrs R. Kelly • Mrs E. Kite
Mrs L. Loud • Mr D. Marsh • Mrs P. Matthews • Mrs M. McGivern
Mrs Neate • Mr and Mrs H. Norris • Mrs Northover • Mrs E. Parsons
Mrs Rawlings • Mr and Mrs Rummings • Mr J. Sage • Mrs Sloper
Mr B. Swan • Mr and Mrs F. Swan • Mr and Mrs G. Swan • Mrs M. White
Mrs M. Young